Our Exciting Earth!

DESERTS

By Claire Romaine

Gareth Stevens
PUBLISHING

Please visit our website, www.garethstevens.com. For a free color catalog of all our high-quality books, call toll free 1-800-542-2595 or fax 1-877-542-2596.

Cataloging-in-Publication Data

Names: Romaine, Claire.
Title: Deserts / Claire Romaine.
Description: New York : Gareth Stevens Publishing, 2018. | Series: Our exciting Earth! | Includes index.
Identifiers: ISBN 9781538209615 (pbk.) | ISBN 9781538209639 (library bound) | ISBN 9781538209622 (6 pack)
Subjects: LCSH: Deserts–Juvenile literature. | Desert ecology–Juvenile literature.
Classification: LCC GB611.R65 2018 | DDC 577.54–dc23

Published in 2018 by
Gareth Stevens Publishing
111 East 14th Street, Suite 349
New York, NY 10003

Editor: Therese Shea
Designer: Bethany Perl

Photo credits: Cover, p. 1, 17 Anton Foltin/Shutterstock.com; p. 5 Ilyshev Dmitry/Shutterstock.com; p. 7 totajla/Shutterstock.com; p. 9 Diego Delso/Wikipedia.org; p. 11 NadyaEugene/Shutterstock.com; p. 13 KajzrPhotography/Shutterstock.com; p. 15 B Norris/Shutterstock.com; p. 19 EcoPrint/Shutterstock.com; p. 21 Jenn_C/Shutterstock.com; p. 23 hadynyah/E+/Getty Images.

Printed in the United States of America

CPSIA compliance information: Batch #CW18GS: For further information contact Gareth Stevens, New York, New York at 1-800-542-2595.

Contents

Let's go to a desert!

Deserts don't
have much water.
They get little rain.

Some deserts
have sand.
Some have rocks.

Some deserts are hot.
Some are cold!

The biggest hot desert is in Africa.

Some plants live
in deserts.
They can live
without much water.

Cactus have tough skin to keep in water.

Some animals live
in deserts.
Some hide
from the sun.

I see donkeys!
They eat plants
for water.

I ride a camel.
Deserts are fun!

Words to Know

cactus

camel

donkey

Index